Practical
Holiday
Entertaining

p^3

This is a P³ Book
This edition published in 2003

P³
Queen Street House
4 Queen Street
Bath BA1 1HE, UK

ISBN: 1-40542-314-5

Manufactured in China

NOTE

Cup measurements in this book are for American cups.
This book also uses imperial and metric measurements. Follow the same units
of measurement throughout; do not mix imperial and metric.
All spoon measurements are level: teaspoons are assumed to be 5 ml, and
tablespoons are assumed to be 15 ml. Unless otherwise stated,
milk is assumed to be whole milk, eggs and individual vegetables such as potatoes
are medium, and pepper is freshly ground black pepper.

The nutritional information provided for each recipe is per serving or per person.
Optional ingredients, variations, or serving suggestions have
not been included in the calculations. The times given for each recipe are an approximate
guide only because the preparation times may differ according to the techniques used by
different people and the cooking times may vary as a result of the type of oven used.

Recipes using raw or very lightly cooked eggs should be
avoided by infants, the elderly, pregnant women, convalescents,
and anyone suffering from an illness.

Contents

Chicken & Leek Soup

This satisfying soup may be served as an entrée. Add rice and bell peppers to make it even more hearty and colorful.

NUTRITIONAL INFORMATION

Calories 183   Sugar 4g
Protein ....21g   Fats 9g
Carbohydrates ....4g Saturates 5g

5 mins   1¼ hrs

SERVES 4–6

I N G R E D I E N T S

2 tbsp butter

12 oz/350 g leeks

12 oz/350 g boneless chicken

5 cups fresh chicken bouillon

1 bouquet garni

8 pitted prunes, halved

½ cup cooked rice and diced bell peppers, optional

salt and white pepper

1 Melt the butter in a large pan. Cut the leeks into 1-inch/ 2.5-cm pieces.

2 Add the chicken and leeks to the pan and cook for 8 minutes.

3 Next add the chicken bouillon and bouquet garni and stir together well.

4 Season the mixture well with salt and freshly ground pepper to taste.

5 Bring the soup to a boil and simmer for 45 minutes.

6 Add the pitted prunes to the pan, with the cooked rice and diced bell peppers if using, and simmer for about 20 minutes.

7 Remove the bouquet garni from the soup and discard. Serve the soup immediately.

VARIATION

Instead of the bouquet garni, you can use a bunch of fresh mixed herbs, tied together with string. Choose herbs such as parsley, thyme, and rosemary.

Navy Bean & Pasta Soup

This soup makes an excellent winter lunch served with warm crusty bread and a slice of cheese.

NUTRITIONAL INFORMATION

Calories 584   Sugars 13g
Protein . . . . .22g   Fat 29g
Carbohydrate . . .63g   Saturates 5g

🥘 3¼ hrs   🕐 1¼ hrs

SERVES 4

I N G R E D I E N T S

1⅓ cups navy beans, soaked for
   3 hours in cold water and drained

4 tbsp olive oil

2 large onions, sliced

3 garlic cloves, chopped

14 oz/400 g canned chopped tomatoes

1 tsp dried oregano

1 tsp tomato paste

3½ cups water

¾ cup dried fusilli or conchigliette

3½ oz/100 g sun-dried tomatoes, drained
   and thinly sliced

1 tbsp chopped fresh cilantro or flatleaf
   parsley

salt and pepper

2 tbsp Parmesan cheese shavings,
   to serve

1 Put the navy beans in a large pan, add sufficient cold water to cover, and bring to a boil over high heat. Boil vigorously for 15 minutes. Drain the beans thoroughly and keep warm.

2 Heat the oil in a pan over medium heat and sauté the onions for 2–3 minutes, or until they are just beginning to change color. Stir in the garlic and cook for 1 minute. Stir in the tomatoes, oregano, and tomato paste.

3 Add the water and the reserved beans to the pan. Bring to a boil, cover, then lower the heat and simmer for about 45 minutes, or until the beans are almost tender.

4 Add the pasta to the pan and season to taste with salt and pepper. Stir in the sun-dried tomatoes, bring back to a boil, partly cover, and simmer for 10 minutes, or until the pasta is tender but still firm to the bite.

5 Stir the cilantro or parsley into the soup. Ladle the soup into a warm tureen, sprinkle with the Parmesan cheese shavings, and serve immediately.

COOK'S TIP

If preferred, place the beans in a pan of cold water and bring to a boil. Remove from the heat and let the beans cool in the water. Drain and rinse before using.

Authentic Guacamole

Guacamole is at its best when freshly made, with enough texture to really taste the avocado. Serve it with vegetable sticks or tortilla chips.

NUTRITIONAL INFORMATION

Calories	212	Sugars	.........1g
Protein	.........2g	Fat	..........21g
Carbohydrate	....3g	Saturates	.......4g

 15 mins   🕐 0 mins

SERVES 4

INGREDIENTS

1 ripe tomato

2 limes

2–3 ripe, small to medium avocados, or 1–2 large ones

¼–½ onion, finely chopped

pinch of ground cumin

pinch of mild chili powder

½–1 fresh green chile, such as jalapeño or serrano, seeded and finely chopped

1 tbsp finely chopped fresh cilantro leaves, plus extra to garnish

salt (optional)

tortilla chips, to serve (optional)

1 Place the tomatoes in a heatproof bowl, pour boiling water over to cover, and let stand for 30 seconds. Drain and plunge into cold water. Peel off the skins. Cut the tomatoes in half, seed, and chop the flesh.

2 Squeeze the juice from the limes into a small bowl. Cut 1 avocado in half around the pit. Twist the 2 halves apart in opposite directions, then remove the pit with a knife. Carefully peel off the skin, dice the flesh, and toss in the bowl of lime juice to prevent the flesh from discoloring. Repeat with the remaining avocados. Mash the avocado flesh fairly coarsely with a fork.

3 Add the onion, tomato, cumin, chili powder, fresh chile, and cilantro to the avocados. If using as a dip for tortilla chips, do not add salt. If using as a dip for vegetable sticks, add salt to taste.

4 To serve the guacamole, transfer it to a serving dish, garnish with finely chopped fresh cilantro, and serve with tortilla chips if using.

COOK'S TIP
Try spooning guacamole into soups, especially chicken or seafood, or spreading it into sandwiches on thick crusty rolls. Spoon guacamole over refried beans and melted cheese, then dig into it with salsa and crisp tortilla chips.

Sticky Ginger Chicken Wings

A finger-licking appetizer of chicken wings or drumsticks, which is ideal for parties (have finger bowls ready).

NUTRITIONAL INFORMATION

Calories	416	Sugars	........5g
Protein	........41g	Fat	..........25g
Carbohydrate	....7g	Saturates	.......7g

15 mins, plus several hrs for marinating | 15 mins

SERVES 4

INGREDIENTS

2 garlic cloves, peeled

1 piece preserved ginger in syrup

1 tsp coriander seeds

2 tbsp preserved ginger syrup

2 tbsp dark soy sauce

1 tbsp lime juice

1 tsp sesame oil

12 chicken wings

lime wedges and fresh cilantro leaves, to garnish

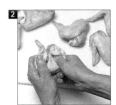

1 Roughly chop the garlic and ginger. In a pestle and mortar, crush the garlic, preserved ginger, and coriander seeds to a paste, gradually working in the ginger syrup, soy sauce, lime juice, and sesame oil.

2 Tuck the pointed tip of each chicken wing underneath the thicker end of the wing to make a neat triangular shape. Place in a large bowl.

3 Add the garlic and ginger paste to the bowl and toss the chicken wings in the mixture to coat evenly. Cover and let marinate in the refrigerator for several hours, or overnight.

4 Arrange the chicken wings in one layer on a foil-lined broiler pan and cook under a preheated medium-hot broiler for 12–15 minutes, turning them occasionally, until golden brown and thoroughly cooked. Alternatively, cook on a lightly oiled barbecue grill over medium-hot coals for 12–15 minutes. Serve garnished with lime wedges and fresh cilantro.

COOK'S TIP

To test if the chicken is cooked, pierce it deeply through the thickest part of the flesh. When fully cooked, the chicken juices are clear, with no trace of pink. If there is any trace of pink, cook for a few more minutes.

Potato & Bean Pâté

This pâté is easy to prepare and may be stored in the refrigerator for up to two days. Serve with small toasts, Melba toast, or crudités.

NUTRITIONAL INFORMATION

Calories 94   Sugars 5g
Protein ....6g   Fat 1g
Carbohydrate ...17g   Saturates 0.2g

5 mins   10 mins

SERVES 4

INGREDIENTS

3½ oz/100 g mealy potatoes, peeled and diced

8 oz/225 g canned mixed beans, such as borlotti beans, lima beans, and kidney beans, drained

1 garlic clove, crushed

2 tsp lime juice

1 tbsp chopped fresh cilantro

2 tbsp lowfat plain yogurt

salt and pepper

fresh cilantro, chopped, to garnish

1 Cook the potatoes in a pan of boiling water for 10 minutes until tender. Drain well and mash.

2 Transfer the potato to a food processor or blender and add the beans, garlic, lime juice, and fresh cilantro. Season the mixture and process for 1 minute to make a smooth puree. Alternatively, put the beans in a bowl with the potato, garlic, lime juice, and cilantro and mash together.

3 If you have used a food processor or blender instead of the hand method, transfer the mixture to a bowl.

4 Add the yogurt and mix well. Spoon the pâté into a serving dish and garnish with the chopped fresh cilantro. Serve at once or let chill.

COOK'S TIP
To make Melba toast, toast ready-sliced bread lightly on both sides under a preheated hot broiler. Remove the crusts. Holding the bread flat, slide a sharp knife through the slice to split it horizontally. Cut into triangles and toast the untoasted side until the edges curl.

Baked Goat Cheese Salad

Scrumptious hot goat cheese and herb croûtes are served with a tossed leafy salad to make an excellent light snack, capturing Provençal flavors.

NUTRITIONAL INFORMATION

Calories 509   Sugars 3g
Protein . . . . .18g   Fat 33g
Carbohydrate . . .35g   Saturates 10g

10 mins   10 mins

SERVES 4

INGREDIENTS

9 oz/250 g mixed salad greens, such as
arugula, mâche, and endive

12 slices French bread, plus extra to serve

extra-virgin olive oil, for brushing

12 thin slices of Provençal goat cheese,
such as Picodon

fresh herbs, such as rosemary, thyme, or
oregano, finely chopped

DRESSING

6 tbsp extra-virgin olive oil

3 tbsp red wine vinegar

½ tsp sugar

½ tsp Dijon mustard

salt and pepper

1 To prepare the salad, rinse the leaves under cold water and pat dry with a dish towel. Wrap in paper towels and put in a plastic bag. Seal tightly and store in the refrigerator, until required.

2 To make the dressing, place all the ingredients in a screw-top jar and shake until well blended. Season with salt and pepper to taste and shake again. Set aside while preparing the croûtes.

3 Under a preheated broiler, toast the slices of French bread on both sides, until they are crisp. Brush a little olive oil on one side of each slice while they are still hot, so the oil is absorbed.

4 Place the croûtes on a cookie sheet and top each with a slice of cheese. Sprinkle the herbs over the cheese and drizzle with olive oil. Bake in a preheated oven, 350°F/180°C, for 5 minutes.

5 While the croûtes are in the oven, place the salad greens in a bowl. Shake the dressing again, pour it over the salad greens and toss together. Divide the salad between 4 plates.

6 Transfer the hot croûtes to the salad greens. Serve immediately with extra slices of French bread.

Crispy Duck with Noodles

A robustly flavored dish that makes a substantial entrée. Serve it with a refreshing cucumber salad or a light vegetable stir-fry.

NUTRITIONAL INFORMATION

Calories 433	Sugars 7g
Protein 25g	Fat 10g
Carbohydrate . . .59g	Saturates 2g

15 mins, plus 1 hr marinating   20–25 mins

SERVES 4

INGREDIENTS

3 duck breasts, total weight about 14 oz/400 g

2 garlic cloves, crushed

1½ tsp chili paste

1 tbsp honey

3 tbsp dark soy sauce

½ tsp five-spice powder

9 oz/250 g rice stick noodles

1 tsp vegetable oil

1 tsp sesame oil

2 scallions, sliced

¾ cup snow peas

2 tbsp tamarind juice

sesame seeds, to garnish

1 Prick the duck breast skin all over with a fork and place the duck breasts in a deep dish.

2 Mix together the garlic, chili paste, honey, soy sauce, and five-spice powder, then pour it over the duck. Turn the breasts over to coat them evenly, then cover and put in the refrigerator to marinate for at least 1 hour.

3 Meanwhile, soak the rice noodles in hot water for 15 minutes. Drain well.

4 Drain the duck breast halves from the marinade and broil on a rack under high heat for about 10 minutes, turning them over occasionally, until they become a rich golden brown. Remove and slice the duck breasts thinly.

5 Heat the vegetable and sesame oils in a skillet and toss the scallions and snow peas in it for 2 minutes. Stir the reserved marinade and tamarind juice into the mixture, and bring to a boil.

6 Add the sliced duck and the noodles to the skillet and toss to heat them through thoroughly. Serve immediately, sprinkled with sesame seeds.

Mixed Nut Roast

Many consider this classic nut roast to be as traditional for vegetarians as turkey is for meat-eaters.

NUTRITIONAL INFORMATION

Calories . . . . . . .628 Sugars 34.1g
Protein . . . . . . .13.8g Fat 43.7g
Carbohydrate . .47.9g Saturates 7.9g

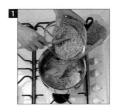

🍴 30 mins   🕐 35 mins

SERVES 4

I N G R E D I E N T S

2 tbsp butter, plus extra for greasing

2 garlic cloves, chopped

1 large onion, chopped

½ cup hazelnuts, toasted and ground

½ cup walnuts, ground

⅓ cup cashews, ground

½ cup pine nuts, toasted and ground

scant 2 cups whole-wheat bread crumbs

1 egg, lightly beaten

2 tbsp chopped fresh thyme

1 cup vegetable bouillon

salt and pepper

C R A N B E R R Y & R E D W I N E   S A U C E

1¾ cups fresh cranberries

½ cup superfine sugar

1¼ cups red wine

1 cinnamon stick

sprigs of fresh thyme, to garnish

Brussels sprouts with buttered chestnuts, to serve

1 Preheat the oven to 350°F/180°C. Grease a loaf pan and line it with waxed paper. Melt the butter in a large pan over medium heat. Add the garlic and onion and cook, stirring, for 3 minutes, until softened. Remove from the heat and stir in the nuts, bread crumbs, egg, thyme, bouillon, and seasoning.

2 Spoon the mixture into the loaf pan and level the surface. Cook in the center of the preheated oven for 30 minutes or until cooked through and golden brown. The loaf is done when a skewer inserted into the center comes out clean. About halfway through the cooking time, make the sauce. Put all the ingredients into a pan and bring to a boil. Reduce the heat and simmer, stirring occasionally, for 15 minutes.

3 To serve, remove the sauce from the heat and discard the cinnamon stick. Remove the nut roast from the oven and turn out. Garnish with thyme; serve with the sauce and Brussels sprouts with buttered chestnuts.

Lentil & Rice Casserole

This is a really hearty dish, perfect for cold days when a filling hot dish is just what you need to keep the winter out.

NUTRITIONAL INFORMATION

Calories	312	Sugars	.........9g
Protein	........20g	Fat	..........2g
Carbohydrate	...51g	Saturates	.....0.4g

15 mins   40 mins

SERVES 4

I N G R E D I E N T S

1 cup split red lentils

generous ¼ cup long-grain rice

5 cups vegetable bouillon

1 leek, cut into chunks

3 garlic cloves, crushed

14 oz/400 g canned chopped tomatoes

1 tsp ground cumin

1 tsp chili powder

1 tsp garam masala

1 red bell pepper, seeded and sliced

3½ oz/100 g small broccoli florets

8 baby corn cobs, halved lengthwise

2 oz/55 g green beans, halved

1 tbsp shredded fresh basil

salt and pepper

sprigs of fresh basil, to garnish

1 Place the lentils, rice, and vegetable bouillon in a large flameproof casserole and cook over low heat, stirring occasionally, for 20 minutes.

2 Add the leek, garlic, tomatoes and their juice, ground cumin, chili powder, garam masala, sliced bell pepper, broccoli, corn cobs, and green beans to the casserole.

3 Bring the mixture to a boil, lower the heat, cover, and simmer for another 10–15 minutes, or until all the vegetables are tender.

4 Add the shredded basil and season with salt and pepper to taste.

5 Garnish with fresh basil sprigs and serve immediately.

VARIATION

You can vary the rice in this recipe—use brown or wild rice, if you prefer.

Pasta & Shrimp Parcels

This is the ideal dish when you have guests because the parcels can be prepared in advance, then put in the oven when you are ready to eat.

NUTRITIONAL INFORMATION

Calories 640	Sugars 1g	
Protein 50g	Fat 29g	
Carbohydrate ...42g	Saturates 4g	

🍤 🍤 🍤

🍲 15 mins   🕐 30 mins

SERVES 4

INGREDIENTS

1 lb/450 g dried fettuccine

⅔ cup ready-made pesto sauce

4 tsp extra-virgin olive oil

1 lb 10 oz/750 g large raw shrimp, peeled and deveined

2 garlic cloves, crushed

½ cup dry white wine

salt and pepper

1 Cut out four 12-inch/30-cm squares of waxed paper.

2 Bring a pan of lightly salted water to a boil. Add the pasta, bring back to a boil, and cook for 2–3 minutes, until just softened. Drain and set aside.

3 Combine the fettuccine and half of the pesto sauce. Spread out the paper squares and put 1 teaspoon of the olive oil in the middle of each. Divide the fettuccine among the squares, then divide the shrimp and place on top of the fettuccine.

4 Combine the remaining pesto sauce and the garlic and spoon it over the shrimp. Season each parcel with salt and pepper to taste and then sprinkle with the white wine.

5 Dampen the edges of the waxed paper and wrap the parcels loosely, twisting the edges to seal.

6 Place the parcels on a cookie sheet and bake in a preheated oven, 400°F/200°C, for 10–15 minutes, until piping hot and the shrimp have changed color. Transfer the parcels to 4 individual serving plates and serve.

COOK'S TIP

Traditionally, these parcels are designed to look like money bags. The resemblance is more effective with waxed paper than with foil.

Stuffed Monkfish Tail

A very impressive-looking dish, which is very simple to prepare. The fish is stuffed with herbs and wrapped in slices of prosciutto.

NUTRITIONAL INFORMATION

Calories 154   Sugars 0g
Protein ....24g   Fat 6g
Carbohydrate ....0g   Saturates 1g

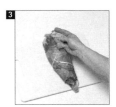

🍲 15 mins   🕐 40 mins

SERVES 6

I N G R E D I E N T S

1 lb 10 oz/750 g monkfish tail, skinned and trimmed

6 slices prosciutto

4 tbsp chopped fresh mixed herbs such as parsley, chives, basil, and sage

1 tsp finely grated lemon zest

2 tbsp olive oil

salt and pepper

TO SERVE

shredded stir-fried vegetables

freshly cooked new potatoes

1 Using a sharp knife, carefully cut down each side of the central bone of the monkfish to leave 2 fillets. Wash and dry the fillets.

2 Lay the prosciutto slices widthwise on a clean counter so that they overlap slightly. Lay the fish fillets lengthwise on top of the prosciutto so that the two cut sides face each other.

3 Mix together the chopped herbs and lemon zest. Season well. Pack this mixture onto the cut surface of one monkfish fillet. Press the 2 fillets together and wrap tightly with the prosciutto slices. Secure with string or toothpicks.

4 Heat the olive oil in a large, ovenproof skillet and place the fish in the skillet, seam-side down first, and brown the wrapped monkfish tail all over.

5 Transfer to a preheated oven and bake at 400°F/200°C for 25 minutes, until the fish is golden and tender. Remove from the oven and let rest for 10 minutes before slicing thickly. Serve with shredded stir-fried vegetables and freshly cooked new potatoes.

COOK'S TIP
It is possible to remove the central bone from a monkfish tail without separating the two fillets completely. This makes it easier to stuff, but takes some practice.

Dover Sole à la Meunière

Dover sole à la meunière, or "in the style of a miller's wife," gets its name from the light dusting of flour that the fish is given before cooking.

NUTRITIONAL INFORMATION

Calories	584	Sugars	.........0g
Protein	........74g	Fat	..........29g
Carbohydrate	...10g	Saturates	......14g

 20 mins · 15 mins

SERVES 4

INGREDIENTS

4 tbsp all-purpose flour

1 tsp salt

4 Dover soles, about 14 oz/400 g each, cleaned and skinned

⅔ cup butter

3 tbsp lemon juice

1 tbsp chopped fresh parsley

¼ preserved lemon, finely chopped (optional)

salt and pepper

lemon wedges and parsley, to garnish

1 Mix the flour with the salt and place on a large plate or tray. Drop the fish into the flour, one at a time, and shake well to remove any excess. Melt 3 tablespoons of the butter in a small pan and use to brush the fish liberally all over.

2 Place under a preheated hot broiler and cook for 5 minutes on each side.

3 Meanwhile, melt the remaining butter in a small pan. Pour cold water into a bowl, large enough to take the bottom of the pan. Keep nearby.

4 Heat the butter until it turns a golden brown and begins to smell nutty.

Remove immediately from the heat and immerse the bottom of the pan in the cold water, to stop the cooking.

5 Put the fish onto individual serving plates, drizzle with the lemon juice, and sprinkle over the parsley, and preserved lemon if using. Season with salt and pepper. Pour over the browned butter and serve immediately, garnished with lemon wedges and parsley sprigs.

COOK'S TIP
If you have a large enough pan (or two) you can cook the floured fish in butter, if you prefer.

Chicken with a Yogurt Crust

A spicy, Indian-style coating is baked around lean chicken to give a full flavor. Serve with a tomato, cucumber, and cilantro relish.

NUTRITIONAL INFORMATION

Calories ....176 Sugars 5g
Protein ....30g Fat 4g
Carbohydrate ....5g Saturates 1g

 10 mins   🕐 35 mins

SERVES 4

INGREDIENTS

1 garlic clove, crushed

1-inch/2.5-cm piece fresh gingerroot, finely chopped

1 fresh green chile, seeded and finely chopped

6 tbsp lowfat plain yogurt

1 tbsp tomato paste

1 tsp ground turmeric

1 tsp garam masala

1 tbsp lime juice

4 boneless, skinless chicken breasts (4¼ oz/125 g each)

salt and pepper

wedges of lime or lemon, to serve

RELISH

4 tomatoes

¼ cucumber

1 small red onion

2 tbsp chopped fresh cilantro

1 Preheat the oven to 375°F/190°C and have ready a mixing bowl and a cookie sheet.

2 Place the garlic, ginger, chile, yogurt, tomato paste, spices, lime juice, and seasoning in a bowl and mix to combine all the ingredients.

3 Wash and pat dry the chicken breasts thoroughly with absorbent paper towels and then place them on the cookie sheet.

4 Spread the spicy yogurt mixture over the chicken and bake in the preheated oven for 30–35 minutes, or until the meat is tender and cooked through.

5 Meanwhile, make the relish. Finely chop the tomatoes, cucumber, and onion, and mix in a bowl with the cilantro. Season with salt and pepper to taste, then cover and chill in the refrigerator until required.

6 Drain the cooked chicken on absorbent paper towels and serve hot with the relish and wedges of lime or lemon. Alternatively, let cool, then chill for at least 1 hour and serve sliced as part of a salad.

Chicken in Green Salsa

Chicken breasts bathed in a fragrant sauce make a delicate dish, perfect for dinner parties. Serve with rice to complete the meal.

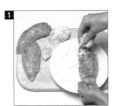

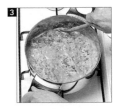

NUTRITIONAL INFORMATION

Calories	349	Sugars 7g
Protein	. . . . .34g	Fat 20g
Carbohydrate	. . .10g	Saturates 12g

 10 mins   🕐 35 mins

SERVES 4

I N G R E D I E N T S

4 chicken breast fillets

flour, for dredging

2–3 tbsp butter or combination of butter and oil

1 lb/450 g mild green salsa or pureed tomatillos

1 cup chicken bouillon

1–2 garlic cloves, finely chopped

3–5 tbsp chopped fresh cilantro

½ fresh green chile, seeded and chopped

½ tsp ground cumin

salt and pepper

TO SERVE

1 cup sour cream

several leaves romaine lettuce, shredded

3–5 scallions, thinly sliced

fresh cilantro, coarsely chopped

1 Sprinkle the chicken with salt and pepper, then dredge in flour. Shake off the excess flour.

2 Melt the butter in a skillet, then add the chicken and cook over medium-high heat, turning once, until they are golden but not cooked through—they will continue to cook slightly in the sauce. Remove from the skillet and set aside.

3 Place the salsa, chicken bouillon, garlic, cilantro, chile, and cumin in a pan and bring to a boil. Reduce the heat to a low simmer. Add the chicken breasts to the sauce, spooning the sauce over the chicken. Continue to cook for up to 15 minutes, or until the chicken is cooked through.

4 Remove the chicken breasts from the pan and season with salt and pepper to taste. Serve with the sour cream, shredded lettuce leaves, sliced scallions, and chopped fresh cilantro.

Spicy Roast Chicken

This chicken dish, ideal for dinner parties, is cooked in the oven—which is very rare in Indian cooking. The chicken can be boned, if desired.

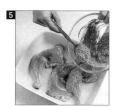

NUTRITIONAL INFORMATION

Calories	586	Sugars	.........6g
Protein	........34g	Fat	..........47g
Carbohydrate	....8g	Saturates	......12g

🍲 5 mins   🕐 50 mins

SERVES 4

I N G R E D I E N T S

scant ½ cup ground almonds

½ cup shredded coconut

⅔ cup oil

1 onion, finely chopped

1 tsp chopped fresh gingerroot

1 tsp crushed garlic

1 tsp chili powder

1½ tsp garam masala

1 tsp salt

⅔ cup plain yogurt

4 chicken quarters, skinned

salad greens, to serve

TO GARNISH

fresh cilantro leaves

1 lemon, cut into wedges

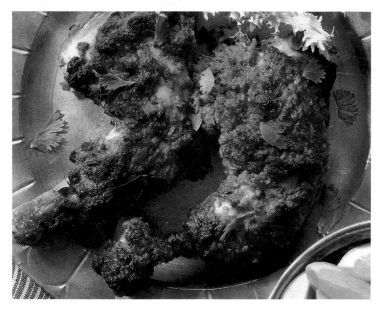

1 In a heavy-bottomed pan, dry roast the ground almonds and coconut over low heat and set aside.

2 Heat the oil in a skillet. Add the onion and cook over low heat, stirring occasionally, until golden brown.

3 Place the ginger, garlic, chili powder, garam masala, and salt in a bowl and mix with the yogurt. Add the almonds and coconut and mix well.

4 Add the onions to the spice mixture, blend, and set aside.

5 Arrange the chicken quarters in a single layer in the bottom of an ovenproof dish. Spoon the spice mixture over the chicken sparingly.

6 Cook in a preheated oven, 325°F/160°C, for 35–45 minutes. Check that the chicken is cooked thoroughly by piercing the thickest part of the meat with the point of a sharp knife or a fine skewer—the juices will run clear when the chicken is cooked through.

7 Garnish with the cilantro and lemon wedges and serve with a salad.

COOK'S TIP

If you want a spicier dish, simply add more chili powder and garam masala.

Traditional Roast Turkey

No Christmas would be complete without a turkey—here it is served with stuffing and complemented by a port and cranberry sauce.

NUTRITIONAL INFORMATION

Calories 713	Sugars 30.8g
Protein 48g	Fat 36.7g
Carbohydrate . .50.8g	Saturates 15.3g

25 mins   3 hrs 20 mins

SERVES 4

I N G R E D I E N T S

6½–7¾ lb/3–3.5 kg oven-ready turkey

6 tbsp olive oil

1 garlic clove, finely chopped

scant ½ cup red wine

S T U F F I N G

3½ oz/100 g white mushrooms

1 onion, chopped

6 tbsp butter

1 garlic clove, chopped

scant 2 cups fresh bread crumbs

2 tbsp finely chopped fresh sage

1 tbsp lemon juice

salt and pepper

P O R T & C R A N B E R R Y S A U C E

½ cup sugar

1 cup port

1¾ cups fresh cranberries

T O S E R V E

roast garlic potatoes

spiced winter vegetables

1 Preheat the oven to 400°F/200°C. To make the stuffing, clean and chop the mushrooms, put them in a pan with the onion and butter and cook for 3 minutes. Remove from the heat and stir in the other ingredients. Rinse the turkey, pat dry with paper towels, fill the neck end with stuffing, and truss with string.

2 Pour the oil into a roasting dish and put the turkey in it. Rub the garlic over the bird and pour the wine over. Roast for 20 minutes. Baste, reduce the heat to 375°F/190°C, and roast for 40 minutes. Baste again and cover with foil. Roast for 2 hours, basting regularly. Check the bird is done by inserting a knife between the legs and body. If the juices run clear, it is done. Remove from the oven and let stand for 25 minutes. Meanwhile, put the sugar, port, and cranberries into a pan. Warm over medium heat until almost boiling. Reduce the heat, simmer for 15 minutes, stirring, then remove from the heat. Serve with the turkey and vegetables.

Honey-Glazed Duck

Chinese-style duck is incredibly easy to prepare, but makes an impressive and truly delicious entrée for a dinner party.

NUTRITIONAL INFORMATION

Calories 230	Sugars 9g
Protein 23g	Fat 9g
Carbohydrate ...14g	Saturates 3g

2¼ hrs   30 mins

SERVES 4

I N G R E D I E N T S

1 tsp dark soy sauce

2 tbsp honey

1 tsp garlic vinegar

2 garlic cloves, crushed

1 tsp ground star anise

2 tsp cornstarch

2 tsp water

2 large boneless duck breasts, about
8 oz/225 g each

TO GARNISH

celery leaves

cucumber wedges

fresh chives

1 Combine the soy sauce, honey, garlic vinegar, garlic, and star anise. Blend the cornstarch with the water to form a smooth paste and stir it into the mixture.

2 Place the duck breasts in a shallow casserole. Brush with the soy marinade, turning them to coat completely. Cover and set aside to marinate in the refrigerator for at least 2 hours or overnight.

3 Remove the duck from the marinade and cook in a preheated oven, 425°F/220°C, for 20–25 minutes, basting frequently with the glaze.

4 Remove the duck from the oven and transfer to a preheated broiler. Broil for about 3–4 minutes to caramelize the top, without charring.

5 Remove the duck from the broiler pan and cut it into thin slices. Arrange the duck slices on a warmed serving dish, garnish with celery leaves, cucumber wedges, and fresh chives, and then serve immediately.

COOK'S TIP

If the duck begins to burn slightly while it is cooking in the oven, cover with foil. Check that the duck breasts are cooked through by inserting the point of a sharp knife into the thickest part of the flesh—the juices should run clear.

Pot Roasted Leg of Lamb

This dish from the Abruzzi region of Italy uses a slow cooking method. The meat absorbs the flavorings and becomes very tender.

NUTRITIONAL INFORMATION

Calories . . . . . . .734 Sugars 6g
Protein . . . . .71g Fat 42g
Carbohydrate . . . .7g Saturates 15g

🔥 🔥 🔥

🥔 35 mins   ⏲ 3 hrs

SERVES 4

I N G R E D I E N T S

3 lb 8 oz/1.6 kg leg of lamb

3–4 sprigs of fresh rosemary

4 oz/115 g bacon strips

4 tbsp olive oil

2–3 garlic cloves, crushed

2 onions, sliced

2 carrots, sliced

2 celery stalks, sliced

1¼ cups dry white wine

1 tbsp tomato paste

1¼ cups bouillon

12 oz/350 g tomatoes, skinned, seeded,
  and cut into fourths

1 tbsp chopped fresh parsley

1 tbsp chopped fresh oregano or marjoram

salt and pepper

sprigs of fresh rosemary, to garnish

1 Wipe the joint of lamb all over, trimming off any excess fat, then season with salt and pepper, rubbing in well. Lay the sprigs of rosemary over the lamb, cover evenly with the bacon strips, and tie in place with string.

2 Heat the oil in a skillet and cook the lamb for about 10 minutes, turning several times. Remove from the skillet.

3 Transfer the oil from the skillet to a large, flameproof casserole and cook the garlic and onions for 3–4 minutes, until beginning to soften. Add the carrots and celery and cook for a few minutes longer.

4 Lay the lamb on top of the vegetables and press down to partly submerge. Pour the wine over the lamb, add the tomato paste, and simmer for about 3–4 minutes. Add the bouillon, tomatoes, and herbs, and season to taste with salt and pepper. Bring back to a boil for another 3–4 minutes.

5 Cover the casserole tightly and cook in a moderate oven, 350°F/180°C, for 2–2½ hours, until very tender.

6 Remove the lamb from the casserole and, if preferred, take off the bacon and herbs along with the string. Keep warm. Strain the juices, skimming off any excess fat, and serve in a pitcher. The vegetables may be arranged around the pot roast or in a serving dish. Garnish with sprigs of fresh rosemary.

Red-Hot Beef with Cashews

Hot and spicy, these quick-cooked beef strips are very tempting.
Serve them with lots of plain rice and cucumber slices to offset the heat.

NUTRITIONAL INFORMATION

Calories	257	Sugars	.........1g
Protein	........32g	Fat	..........13g
Carbohydrate	....3g	Saturates	.......4g

2¼–3¼ hrs   10 mins

SERVES 4

I N G R E D I E N T S

1 lb 2 oz/500 g boneless, lean beef sirloin, thinly sliced

1 tsp vegetable oil

1 tsp sesame oil

4 tbsp unsalted cashews

1 scallion, thickly sliced diagonally

cucumber slices, to garnish

M A R I N A D E

1 tbsp sesame seeds

1 garlic clove, chopped

1 tbsp finely chopped fresh gingerroot

1 fresh, red bird-eye chile, chopped

2 tbsp dark soy sauce

1 tsp red curry paste

1 Cut the beef into ½-inch/1-cm wide strips. Place the strips in a large, nonmetallic bowl.

2 To make the marinade, dry-cook the sesame seeds in a heavy pan over medium heat for 2–3 minutes.

3 Place the seeds in a mortar with the garlic, ginger, and chile and grind to a smooth paste with a pestle. Add the soy sauce and curry paste and mix well.

4 Spoon the paste over the beef strips and toss well to coat the meat evenly. Cover and set aside to marinate in the refrigerator for 2–3 hours or overnight.

5 Heat a heavy skillet or ridged grill pan until very hot, then brush with vegetable oil. Add the beef strips and cook quickly, turning frequently, until lightly browned. Remove from the heat and spoon into a pile on a warmed serving dish.

6 Heat the sesame oil in a small pan and cook the cashews, until golden. Add the scallion and stir-fry for 30 seconds. Sprinkle the mixture onto the beef and serve garnished with cucumber.

Christmas Pudding

This timeless, classic pudding is an essential part of the Christmas table. Make it well in advance, because it needs to chill for at least two weeks.

NUTRITIONAL INFORMATION

Calories	1273	Sugars	.....150.4g
Protein	.......20.6g	Fat	..........51g
Carbohydrate	..197g	Saturates	....25.3g

2¼ hrs   8 hrs + 2–8 weeks to chill

SERVES 4

INGREDIENTS

1⅓ cups currants

scant 1⅓ cups raisins

scant 1¼ cups golden raisins

⅔ cup sweet sherry

¾ cup butter, plus extra for greasing

generous ¾ cup brown sugar

4 eggs, beaten

generous 1 cup self-rising flour

scant 2 cups fresh white or whole-wheat bread crumbs

⅓ cup blanched almonds, chopped

juice of 1 orange

grated zest of ½ orange

grated zest of ½ lemon

½ tsp ground allspice

holly leaves, to decorate

1 Put the currants, raisins, and golden raisins into a glass bowl and pour over the sherry. Let soak for at least 2 hours.

2 Mix the butter and sugar in a bowl. Beat in the eggs, then fold in the flour. Stir in the soaked fruit and sherry with the bread crumbs, almonds, orange juice and zest, lemon zest, and allspice. Grease an ovenproof bowl and press the mixture into it, leaving a gap of 1 inch/2.5 cm at the top. Cut a circle of waxed paper 1½ inches/3 cm larger than the top of the bowl, grease with butter, and place over the pudding. Secure with string, then top with 2 layers of foil. Place the pudding in a pan filled with boiling water which reaches two-thirds of the way up the bowl. Reduce the heat and simmer for 6 hours, topping up the water when necessary.

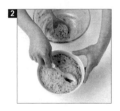

3 Remove from the heat and let cool. Renew the waxed paper and foil and refrigerate for 2–8 weeks. To reheat, steam for 2 hours as before. Decorate with holly and serve.

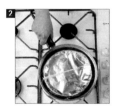

Italian Bread Pudding

This deliciously rich dessert is cooked with cream and apples and is delicately flavored with orange.

NUTRITIONAL INFORMATION

Calories 387   Sugars 31g
Protein . . . . .8g   Fat 20g
Carbohydrate . . .45g   Saturates 12g

45 mins   🕐 25 mins

SERVES 4

I N G R E D I E N T S

1 tbsp butter

2 small dessert apples, peeled, cored, and
   sliced into rings

½ cup granulated sugar

2 tbsp white wine

4 thick slices of bread (about 4 oz/115 g),
   crusts removed (day-old baguette is ideal)

1¼ cups light cream

2 eggs, beaten

pared rind of 1 orange, cut into short,
   thin sticks

1 Lightly grease a 5-cup deep casserole
   with the butter.

2 Arrange the apple rings in the bottom
   of the dish. Sprinkle half of the sugar
over the apples.

3 Pour the wine over the apples. Add
   the bread slices, pushing them down
with your hands to flatten them slightly.

4 Mix the cream with the eggs, the
   remaining sugar, and the orange rind
and pour the mixture over the bread. Set
aside to soak for 30 minutes.

5 Transfer the dessert to an oven
   preheated to 350°F/180°C and bake
for 25 minutes, until golden and set.
Remove from the oven, set aside to cool
slightly, and serve warm.

Orange & Almond Cake

This light and tangy citrus cake from Sicily is better eaten as a dessert than as a cake. It is especially good served after a large meal.

NUTRITIONAL INFORMATION

Calories 399   Sugars 20g
Protein . . . . .8g   Fat 31g
Carbohydrate . . .23g   Saturates 13g

🍰 25 mins   🕐 40 mins

SERVES 8

INGREDIENTS

melted butter, for greasing

4 eggs, separated

⅔ cup superfine sugar, plus 2 tsp for the cream

finely grated zest and juice of 2 oranges

finely grated zest and juice of 1 lemon

generous 1 cup ground almonds

scant ¼ cup self-rising flour

generous ¾ cup light cream, for whipping

1 tsp cinnamon

scant ¼ cup slivered almonds, toasted

confectioners' sugar, to dust

1 Grease and line the bottom of a 7-inch/18-cm round, deep cake pan.

2 Whisk the egg yolks with the sugar until thick and creamy. Whisk in half the orange zest and all the lemon zest.

VARIATION

You could serve this cake with a syrup. Boil the juice and finely grated zest of 2 oranges, 6 tbsp superfine sugar, and 2 tbsp of water for 5–6 minutes, until slightly thickened. Stir in 1 tbsp of orange liqueur just before serving.

 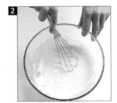 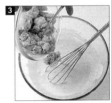

3 Mix the orange and lemon juice with the ground almonds and stir into the egg yolk mixture. It will become quite runny at this point. Fold in the flour.

4 Whisk the egg whites until stiff and gently fold into the egg yolk mixture.

5 Pour the cake mixture into the pan and bake the cake in a preheated oven, at 350°F/180°C, for 35–40 minutes, or until golden and springy to the touch. Let the cake cool in the pan for 10 minutes

and then turn it out. The cake is likely to sink slightly at this stage.

6 Whip the cream to form soft peaks. Stir in the remaining orange zest, the cinnamon, and the 2 teaspoons of sugar.

7 Once the cake is cold, cover with the almonds, dust with confectioners' sugar, and serve with the cream.

Almond Slices

A mouthwatering dessert that is sure to impress your guests, especially if it is served with whipped cream.

NUTRITIONAL INFORMATION

Calories	416	Sugars	.......37g
Protein	........11g	Fat	.........26g
Carbohydrate	...38g	Saturates	......12g

 15 mins   45 mins

SERVES 8

INGREDIENTS

½ cup sweet butter, plus extra for greasing

⅔ cup ground almonds

1½ cups milk powder

1 cup superfine sugar

½ tsp saffron strands

3 eggs, beaten

scant ¼ cup slivered almonds, to decorate

1 Lightly grease a shallow 9-inch/23-cm ovenproof dish with butter.

2 Place the ground almonds, milk powder, sugar, and saffron in a large mixing bowl and stir to mix well.

3 Melt the butter in a small pan. Pour the melted butter over the dry ingredients and mix well.

COOK'S TIP

These almond slices are best eaten hot, but they may also be served cold. They can be made a day or even a week in advance and reheated. They also freeze beautifully.

4 Add the beaten eggs to the mixture and stir to blend well.

5 Spread the cake mixture in the prepared dish and bake in a preheated oven, 325°F/160°C, for 45 minutes. Test whether the cake is cooked through by piercing with the tip of a sharp knife or a skewer—it will come out clean if it is cooked thoroughly. If not, cook for an additional 5 minutes and test again.

6 Cut the almond cake into slices. Decorate the almond slices with slivered almonds and transfer to serving plates. Serve hot or cold.

Rum Truffles

Truffles are always popular. They make a fabulous gift or, served with coffee, they are a perfect end to a meal.

🍮 45 mins   🕐 5 mins

MAKES 20

I N G R E D I E N T S

4½ oz/125 g dark chocolate

small knob of butter

about 2 tbsp rum

½ cup shredded coconut

3½ oz/100 g cake crumbs

6 tbsp confectioners' sugar

2 tbsp unsweetened cocoa

1 Break the chocolate into pieces and place in a bowl with the butter. Set the bowl over a pan of gently simmering water and stir until melted and combined.

2 Remove from the heat and beat in the rum. Stir in the shredded coconut, cake crumbs, and two-thirds of the confectioners' sugar. Beat until combined. Add a little extra rum if the mixture is stiff.

3 Roll the mixture into small balls and place them on a sheet of baking parchment. Chill until firm.

4 Sift the remaining confectioners' sugar onto a large plate. Sift the cocoa onto another plate. Roll half of the truffles in the confectioners' sugar until coated, then roll the remaining truffles in the cocoa.

5 Place the truffles in paper candy cases and chill in the refrigerator until required.

VARIATION
Make the truffles with white chocolate and replace the rum with coconut liqueur or milk, if you prefer. Roll them in unsweetened cocoa or dip in melted light chocolate.

Chocolate Fondue

This is a fun dessert to serve at the end of a meal. Prepare in advance, then simply warm through before serving.

10 mins   5 mins

SERVES 4

I N G R E D I E N T S

8 oz/225 g dark chocolate

generous ¾ cup heavy cream

2 tbsp brandy

T O   S E R V E

selection of fruit

white and pink marshmallows

sweet cookies

1 Break the chocolate into small pieces and place in a small pan with the heavy cream.

2 Heat the mixture gently, stirring constantly, until the chocolate has melted and blended with the cream.

3 Remove the pan from the heat and stir in the brandy.

4 Pour into a fondue pot or a small flameproof dish and keep warm, preferably over a small burner.

5 Serve with a selection of fruit, marshmallows, and cookies for dipping. The fruit and marshmallows can be spiked on fondue forks, wooden skewers, or ordinary forks, for dipping into the chocolate fondue.

COOK'S TIP

To prepare the fruit for dipping, cut larger fruit into bite-size pieces. Fruits that discolor, such as bananas, apples, and pears, should be dipped in a little lemon juice as soon as they are cut.